**ESSENTIAL ELEMENTS**

**E**

**GUITAR ENSEMBLES**

# BOSSA NOVA

T0078932

## CONTENTS

Arrangements by Chip Henderson

ISBN 978-1-4234-6806-6

**HAL•LEONARD® CORPORATION**

7777 W. BLUEMOUND RD. P.O. BOX 13819 MILWAUKEE, WI 53213

For all works contained herein:
Unauthorized copying, arranging, adapting, recording, Internet posting, public performance,
or other distribution of the printed music in this publication is an infringement of copyright.
Infringers are liable under the law.

Visit Hal Leonard Online at
**www.halleonard.com**

# ÁGUA DE BEBER
## (Water to Drink)

English Words by Norman Gimbel
Portuguese Words by Vinicius De Moraes
Music by Antonio Carlos Jobim

Copyright © 1961, 1970 by EDIZIONI CAMPIDOGLIO - Roma Via D. Montverde, 11, Italy
English Lyrics Copyright © 1965 BEXHILL MUSIC CORP. and NORMAN GIMBEL for the World
Copyright Renewed
This arrangement Copyright © 2010 by EDIZIONI CAMPIDOGLIO, BEXHILL MUSIC CORP. and NORMAN GIMBEL
All Rights Administered by GIMBEL MUSIC GROUP, INC. (P.O. Box 15221, Beverly Hills, CA 90209 USA), CORCOVADO MUSIC CORP., New York, NY and VM ENTERPRISES, INC., New York, NY
All Rights Reserved   Used by Permission

# BLACK ORPHEUS

Words and Music by Luiz Bonfa

Copyright © 1968 by Chappell & Co.
Copyright Renewed
This arrangement Copyright © 2010 by Chappell & Co.
International Copyright Secured   All Rights Reserved

# CALL ME

Words and Music by Tony Hatch

Copyright © 1965 WELBECK MUSIC LTD.
Copyright Renewed
This arrangement Copyright © 2010 WELBECK MUSIC LTD.
All Rights for the United States and Canada Controlled and Administered by SONGS OF UNIVERSAL, INC.
All Rights Reserved   Used by Permission

# DINDI

Music by Antonio Carlos Jobim
Portuguese Lyrics by Aloysio de Oliveira
English Lyrics by Ray Gilbert

Copyright © 1965 Antonio Carlos Jobim and Aloysio de Oliveira
Copyright Renewed, Assigned to Corcovado Music Corp. and Ipanema Music Corp.
This arrangement Copyright © 2010 Corcovado Music Corp. and Ipanema Music Corp.
International Copyright Secured  All Rights Reserved

# THE GIRL FROM IPANEMA
## (Garôta de Ipanema)

Music by Antonio Carlos Jobim
English Words by Norman Gimbel
Original Words by Vinicius de Moraes

Copyright © 1963 ANTONIO CARLOS JOBIM and VINICIUS DE MORAES, Brazil
Copyright Renewed 1991 and Assigned to SONGS OF UNIVERSAL, INC. and NEW THUNDER MUSIC, INC.
English Words Renewed 1991 by NORMAN GIMBEL for the World and Assigned to NEW THUNDER MUSIC, INC. Administered by
GIMBEL MUSIC GROUP, INC. (P.O. Box 15221, Beverly Hills, CA 90209-1221 USA)
This arrangement Copyright © 2010 SONGS OF UNIVERSAL, INC. and NEW THUNDER MUSIC, INC.
All Rights Reserved   Used by Permission

# HOW INSENSITIVE
## (Insensatez)

Music by Antonio Carlos Jobim
Original Words by Vinicius de Moraes
English Words by Norman Gimbel

Copyright © 1963, 1964 ANTONIO CARLOS JOBIM and VINICIUS DE MORAES, Brazil
Copyright Renewed and Assigned to SONGS OF UNIVERSAL, INC. and NEW THUNDER MUSIC, INC.
This arrangement Copyright © 2010 SONGS OF UNIVERSAL, INC. and NEW THUNDER MUSIC, INC.
All Rights for NEW THUNDER MUSIC, INC. Administered by GIMBEL MUSIC GROUP, INC. (P.O. Box 15221, Beverly Hills, CA 90209-1221 USA)
All Rights Reserved   Used by Permission

# LITTLE BOAT

Original Lyric by Ronaldo Boscoli
English Lyric by Buddy Kaye
Music by Roberto Menescal

Copyright © 1963 EDITIONS SACHA S.A.R.L.
Copyright Renewed
This arrangement Copyright © 2010 EDITIONS SACHA S.A.R.L.
All Rights for the U.S. and Canada Controlled and Administered by SONGS OF UNIVERSAL, INC.
All Rights Reserved   Used by Permission

# A MAN AND A WOMAN
## (Un Homme et une Femme)

from A MAN AND A WOMAN
Original Words by Pierre Barouh
English Words by Jerry Keller
Music by Francis Lai

Copyright © 1966 EDITIONS SARAVAH, Paris, France
Copyright Renewed
This arrangement Copyright © 2010 EDITIONS SARAVAH
All Rights in the U.S. and Canada Controlled and Administered by UNIVERSAL MUSIC CORP.
All Rights Reserved   Used by Permission

# ONCE I LOVED
## (Amor em Paz) (Love in Peace)

Music by Antonio Carlos Jobim
Portuguese Lyrics by Vinicius de Moraes
English Lyrics by Ray Gilbert

Copyright © 1963 Antonio Carlos Jobim and Vinicius de Moraes
English lyrics Copyright © 1965 Ipanema Music Corp.
Copyright Renewed, Assigned to Corcovado Music Corp., Ipanema Music Corp. and VM Enterprises, Inc.
This arrangement Copyright © 2010 Corcovado Music Corp., Ipanema Music Corp. and VM Enterprises, Inc.
International Copyright Secured   All Rights Reserved

# ONLY TRUST YOUR HEART

Words by Sammy Cahn
Music by Benny Carter

Copyright © 1964 UNIVERSAL MUSIC CORP.
Copyright Renewed
This arrangement Copyright © 2010 UNIVERSAL MUSIC CORP.
All Rights Reserved   Used by Permission

# QUIET NIGHTS OF QUIET STARS
## (Corcovado)
English Words by Gene Lees
Original Words and Music by Antonio Carlos Jobim

Copyright © 1962, 1964 ANTONIO CARLOS JOBIM
Copyright Renewed
This arrangement Copyright © 2010 ANTONIO CARLOS JOBIM
All Rights for English Speaking Countries Controlled and Administered by SONGS OF UNIVERSAL, INC.
All Rights Reserved   Used by Permission

*D.C. al Coda*

# TRISTE

By Antonio Carlos Jobim

Copyright © 1967, 1968 Antonio Carlos Jobim
Copyright Renewed
This arrangement Copyright © 2010 Antonio Carlos Jobim
Published by Corcovado Music Corp.
International Copyright Secured   All Rights Reserved

# WATCH WHAT HAPPENS

from THE UMBRELLAS OF CHERBOURG
Music by Michel Legrand
Original French Text by Jacques Demy
English Lyrics by Norman Gimbel

Copyright © 1964 PRODUCTIONS MICHEL LEGRAND and PRODUCTIONS FRANCIS LEMARQUE
Copyright © 1965 UNIVERSAL - SONGS OF POLYGRAM INTERNATIONAL, INC. and JONWARE MUSIC CORP.
Copyright Renewed; English words Renewed 1993 by NORMAN GIMBEL and Assigned to GIMBEL MUSIC GROUP, INC. (P.O. Box 15221, Beverly Hills, CA 90209 USA)
This arrangement Copyright © 2010 UNIVERSAL - SONGS OF POLYGRAM INTERNATIONAL, INC., JONWARE MUSIC CORP. and GIMBEL MUSIC GROUP
All Rights Reserved    Used by Permission

# WAVE

Words and Music by Antonio Carlos Jobim

Copyright © 1967, 1968 Antonio Carlos Jobim
Copyright Renewed
This arrangement Copyright © 2010 Antonio Carlos Jobim
Published by Corcovado Music Corp.
International Copyright Secured   All Rights Reserved

# DESAFINADO

Original Text by Newton Mendonça
Music by Antonio Carlos Jobim

© Copyright 1959 (Renewed), 1962 (Renewed) Editora Musical Arapua, Sao Paulo, Brazil
This arrangement Copyright © 2010 Editora Musical Arapua
Corcovado Music Corp., New York, NY, and Bendig Music Corp., Water Mill, NY control all publication rights for the U.S.A.
All Rights for Canada Controlled by Hollis Music, Inc., New York, NY
International Copyright Secured
All Rights Reserved Including Public Performance For Profit
Used by Permission

32